EDGE
BOOKS™

All ABOUT Dogs

MUTTS

by Tammy Gagne

Consultant: Jennifer Zablotny, DVM
Member, American Veterinary
Medical Association

Capstone press®
Mankato, Minnesota

Edge Books are published by Capstone Press,
151 Good Counsel Drive, P.O. Box 669, Mankato, Minnesota 56002.
www.capstonepress.com

Library of Congress Cataloging-in-Publication Data
Gagne, Tammy.
    Mutts / by Tammy Gagne.
    p. cm. — (Edge books. All about dogs)
    Includes bibliographical references and index.
    Summary: "Describes the history, physical features, temperament, and care
of mutts" — Provided by publisher.
    ISBN-13: 978-1-4296-2303-2 (hardcover)
    ISBN-10: 1-4296-2303-9 (hardcover)
    1. Mutts (Dogs) — Juvenile literature. I. Title.
SF426.5.G34 2009
636.7 — dc22   2008028887

Editorial Credits
Erika Shores, editor; Veronica Bianchini, designer; Marcie Spence,
    photo researcher; Marcy Morin, photo shoot scheduler

Photo Credits: All photos by Capstone Press/Karon Dubke except:
AP Images/Enric Marti, 11
Cheryl A. Ertelt, 19
Getty Images Inc./Paul J. Richards/AFP, 8–9; Yaov Lemmer/AFP, 13
iStockphoto/sdart, 26; X2Photo, 15
Shutterstock/Cynthia Kidwell, 7; Mircea Bezergheanu, 16–17

1 2 3 4 5 6 14 13 12 11 10 09

Table of Contents

CHAPTER 1

MIXED-UP DOGS

Purebred dogs can fetch high prices. People pay hundreds, even thousands of dollars for Yorkshire terriers, Labrador retrievers, or Chihuahuas. But you don't have to spend a lot of money to own a good dog. Mutts can also make great pets.

Mutts are dogs with many breeds in their backgrounds. Most dogs of the same breed look and act alike. Mutts, on the other hand, are different from each other in looks and behavior. They can be large or small. Some mutts have long, shaggy coats. Others have soft, smooth coats. One mutt might be calm. Another can be full of energy.

Mutts come in all sizes and colors. No two mutts look exactly the same.

Hybrids Versus Mutts

When one dog breed is mated with another, the puppies are called hybrids. A cockapoo is a popular hybrid created by mating a poodle with a cocker spaniel. Another hybrid is the Labradoodle. A Labrador retriever is mated with a poodle. But mutts aren't hybrids. Mutts have more than two breeds in their backgrounds.

A mutt may have several different purebreds in its family tree. A mutt may also come from a long line of other mutts. Both mutts and hybrids are sometimes called mixed breeds.

A Labradoodle is a mix of the Labrador retriever and the standard poodle breeds.

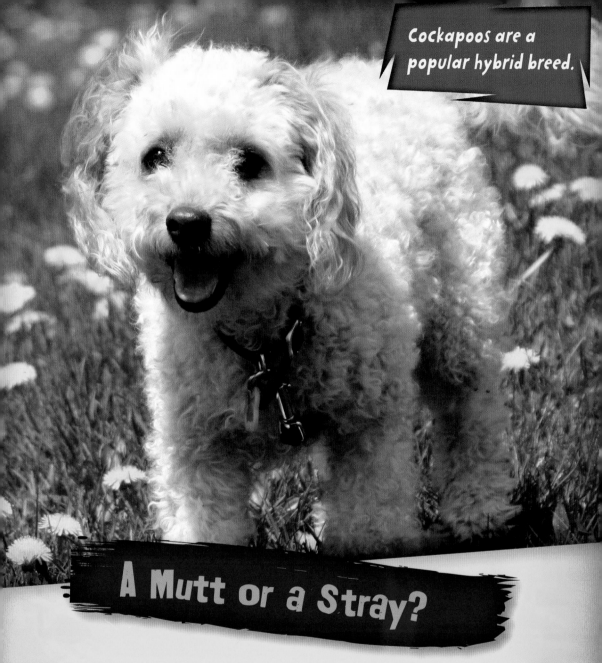

A Mutt or a Stray?

Some people confuse mutts with stray dogs. Stray dogs live on the streets. They are often hurt or killed by cars and wild animals. Many strays end up in animal shelters. Some stray dogs are mutts. But other strays are purebred dogs that have been abandoned by their owners or become lost.

A mutt is sometimes called a Heinz 57. The H. J. Heinz company once used the term to stand for the 57 varieties of food it sold. Heinz 57 became a popular way to describe a dog with an unknown breed background.

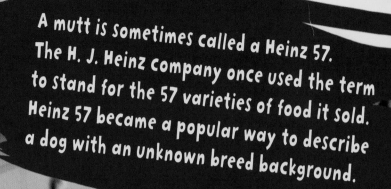

Many of the dogs found in animal shelters are mutts.

In Search of a Good Dog

Some people look for dogs with the qualities of more than one breed. Mutts offer these dog lovers the best of both worlds. If you think a mutt is right for you, consider adopting one.

A local animal shelter is a great place to find a dog in need of a good home. Adopting an animal from a shelter gives it a second chance at a happy life.

Mutts are also sometimes advertised in newspapers or at pet supply stores.

CHAPTER 2

ALL ABOUT DOGS

To best understand mutts, it's important to look at the history of all dogs. The wolf is the dog's closest relative. But wolves are wild. Dogs were the first **domesticated** animals. Dogs and people have lived together for at least 14,000 years. Tame dogs helped their owners hunt. Early dogs were also valued as pets.

Long before dogs became pets, however, they roamed wild. Just like wolves, dogs are pack animals. Pack animals do everything together. They hunt, eat, and rest as a group. Today many pet dogs consider their human owners to be members of their pack.

domesticated — tamed so that it can live with or be used by humans

Ancient Egyptians used dogs to help them hunt.

Keen Senses

At birth, all puppies are blind and deaf. Their eyes and ears open slowly during the first two weeks of life. An adult dog's ability to hear and locate sounds is far better than a person's. Some scientists think dogs can hear sounds from four times the distance a person can.

A dog's amazing sense of smell sets it apart from humans and many other animals. A dog's sense of smell is about 50 times stronger than a person's. If a dog could talk, it would likely describe its surroundings by the scents rather than by the sights or sounds.

EDGE FACT

Whether dogs are purebreds or mutts, all dogs have some things in common. Dogs typically have 321 bones in their bodies. Adult dogs also have 42 teeth.

Puppies don't open their eyes until they are a week or two old.

Breeding For a Purpose

Throughout history, people have bred dogs for different reasons. Most breeds were developed to suit a particular need. Some breeds, like cocker spaniels, help hunters find birds. Others, such as beagles, are better at tracking land animals. Collies are suited for herding livestock. Bloodhounds were bred to be hunting dogs. Now they are raised to search for missing people. Many small breeds are simply valued as companions by their owners.

Today, the American Kennel Club (AKC) recognizes more than 150 different pure breeds. Mutts may never receive the attention purebreds get. But mutts and purebreds share one very important quality. They are wonderful pets for the right people. The bond between dogs and humans is truly unique.

EDGE FACT

Wolves and dogs can produce hybrid offspring. Some states outlaw owning wolf hybrids. Many people fear that these dogs are too wild to be safe pets.

A Bloodhound's excellent sense of smell is used to search for and rescue missing people.

CHAPTER 3

NO TWO MUTTS ARE THE SAME

Breeders of purebred dogs work hard to make sure their dogs match a breed standard. The breed standard is a detailed description of how the breed should look. Mutts have no such common qualities. They come in all shapes, sizes, and colors. Each time a **litter** of mutts is born, the puppies may look like the mother, father, or a mix of both dogs. A mutt puppy may also look different from its parents and its littermates.

Many people believe that mutts should not be bred on purpose. Too little is known about most mutts' family histories to predict the qualities their puppies will have. Breeders of purebred dogs are much more likely to know what their next litter of puppies will be like.

litter — a group of young born to one mother at the same time

Mutt puppies born in the same litter can be many different colors.

17

At Work And Play

Mutts are not allowed to compete in dog shows. However, they do participate in other organized events. Some mutts compete in obedience and **agility** contests. Obedience contests allow dogs and their owners to show off the dogs' skills at following commands. At agility contests, dogs run over ramps and other equipment as quickly as possible.

Other mutts work as therapy dogs. Therapy dogs comfort people during difficult times. These dogs visit patients in hospitals or people living in nursing homes.

EDGE FACT

A dog named Benji is a very famous mutt. The *Benji* movies feature stories of this brave mutt and his adventures. The first Benji movie was released in 1974.

agility — the ability to move quickly

Mutts can be just as skilled in agility contests as purebred dogs.

CHAPTER 4

CARING FOR A MUTT

Mutts cost far less than purebred dogs. They may even be free. No matter what a dog costs, though, owning one is a big responsibility.

Training a Mutt

Mutts need the same kind of training as purebred dogs. All dogs respond best to positive training. This means rewarding them for what they do right instead of punishing them for what they do wrong. Some owners enjoy giving their dogs treats as rewards. The best rewards of all, though, are praise and affection. Nearly all dogs enjoy knowing they have pleased their owners.

Using a treat to reward your mutt will help it learn new commands.

The amount of food you feed your mutt is determined by its size and activity level.

Start training your mutt as soon as you bring it home. You may have heard the saying, "You can't teach an old dog new tricks." Luckily, this is not true. Even older mutts can learn how to behave properly. Like people, dogs can continue learning all their lives. Owners just need more patience when training older pets.

Feeding A Mutt

Feed your dog high-quality pet food. Follow the package directions for the feeding amount based on your dog's weight. Because mutts can differ so much in size, you may want to choose a food made specifically for smaller or larger dogs. Foods for very active dogs and overweight dogs are also available.

Mutts with long coats
need daily grooming.

Dogs can also eat many human foods. Most lean meats and vegetables are just as healthy for your mutt as they are for you. No matter what food you use, you shouldn't overfeed your dog. Two foods that should never be given to dogs are onions and chocolate. These foods can make a dog very sick.

Grooming A Mutt

The amount of grooming your mutt needs will depend on its coat type. If it has long or silky fur, you will need to brush the dog once a day. Short hair may only need brushing once a week. Brushing does more than keep your pet's coat free of tangles. It also removes dirt and dead hair from your dog's coat. The more you brush your mutt, the less fur it will shed onto your furniture and clothing.

Like brushing, how often you bathe your mutt depends on the type of fur it has. In general, you should bathe your dog as often as once a month. Be sure to rinse the shampoo completely from the dog's fur. Any soap left in the fur could cause dry skin and itchiness. If your dog's coat stays fairly clean, it might need a bath just once every few months.

Bathing a mutt keeps its coat healthy and smelling good.

Brushing your dog's teeth
helps prevent gum disease.

Finally, don't forget to brush your mutt's teeth. Keeping your dog's mouth free of plaque will help prevent gum disease. Bacteria in your dog's mouth can spread through its body and lead to health problems. Only use toothpastes made for dogs. Human products can make dogs sick.

Keeping a Mutt Healthy

All dogs should visit a veterinarian at least once a year. A veterinarian, or vet, is a doctor who treats animals. During the exam, your dog will receive **vaccinations** and have its skin and joints checked. Your dog's yearly vet visit is a time to discuss any problems you are having with your mutt. A vet can also give you information about other areas of pet care, such as training and feeding.

Many owners choose to have a vet spay or neuter their mutt. These simple operations prevent dogs from having puppies. Spaying and neutering helps control the pet population. It also lowers a dog's risk for many health problems, including cancer.

With proper care, mutts can live long and happy lives. These dogs don't come with fancy pedigrees. But they can bring a lot of love to their owners' lives. After all, that's the most important job any dog has.

vaccination — medicine that protects animals from disease

Mutts make terrific pets for all kinds of owners.

Glossary

agility (uh-JI-luh-tee) — the ability to move fast and easily

breed (BREED) — a certain kind of animal within an animal group; breed also means to mate and raise a certain kind of animal.

breeder (BREE-duhr) — someone who breeds and raises dogs or other animals

domesticated (duh-MESS-tuh-kay-tuhd) — tamed so that it can live with or be used by humans

litter (LIT-ur) — a group of animals born to one mother at the same time

vaccination (vak-suh-NAY-shun) — a shot of medicine that protects animals from a disease

Read More

Bolan, Sandra. *Caring for Your Mutt.* Our Best Friends. Pittsburgh: ElDorado Ink, 2008.

Jeffrey, Laura S. *Dogs: How to Choose and Care for a Dog.* American Humane Pet Care Library. Berkeley Heights, N.J.: Enslow, 2004.

Stone, Lynn M. *Mutts.* Eye to Eye with Dogs. Vero Beach, Fla.: Rourke, 2009.

Internet Sites

FactHound offers a safe, fun way to find educator-approved Internet sites related to this book.

Here's what you do:

1. Visit *www.facthound.com*
2. Choose your grade level.
3. Begin your search.

This book's ID number is 9781429623032.

FactHound will fetch the best sites for you!

Index